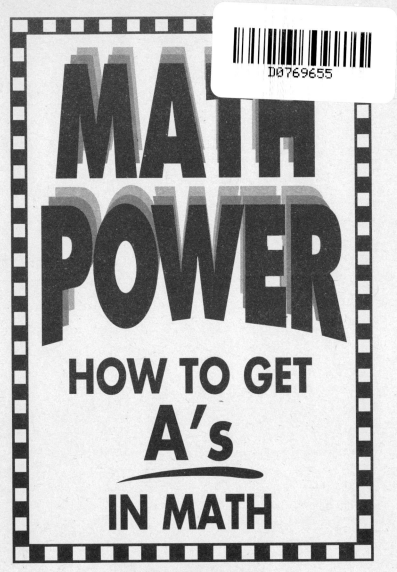

MATH POWER

HOW TO GET A's IN MATH

Denise Bieniek

illustrated by Barbara Levy

Troll Associates

Contents

Mathematics is a very important part of our everyday lives. For example, when a friend asks how you think you did on a science test, your reply is an estimate. When you compare the merits of one team in the NBA over another, you are using statistics. When you take an umbrella with you in the morning based on the clouds outside, you are dealing in probability. We use addition, subtraction, multiplication, and division when shopping. We also use percents and decimals when dealing with money. Telling time and scheduling the events in our day also involve mathematics.

Since many of the things we do each day seem to use math, it's a good idea to know the basics. This book uses a simple and straightforward approach to help you master important math skills. After you've worked through the answers for a particular section, have a friend try some of the problems. This teamwork will not only make math practice more fun, but will sharpen your skills even further.

Population Explosion

The census takers are getting ready for the next national census, which will be in the year 2000. They are looking for counties in which to test the new census form. Each group of towns in each county must have fewer than 250,000 people.

Add the following population counts for the towns in each county below to find out which ones may be used in the testing.

1.	Mountain Lake Kenosha Centerville	52,360 128,181 85,183	6.	Shawnee Bellmore Hillside	160,976 50,580 38,816
2.	Charlottesville New City Yorktown	40,341 79,294 111,183	7.	Bay Head Saint Johns Santa Clara	101,115 83,829 81,608
3.	Blair Pike Lawrence	130,542 27,966 96,246	8.	Denville Commack Appleton	107,714 97,624 93,497
4.	Genesee Selbyville Ridge City	60,060 33,683 154,429	9.	Belleville Mendocino Sawyer	182,120 80,345 64,415
5.	Troy Tallahassee Yardlay	1,909 15,210 12,033	10.	Santana McKinley Pikesville	98,928 60,686 45,235

On a separate piece of paper, answer the following word problems.

1. On Monday, the hot dog stand sold 2,346 hot dogs and 9,780 sodas. On Tuesday, the stand sold 2,500 hot dogs. On Wednesday, the stand sold 1,980 hot dogs and 457 sodas. The amount of hot dogs sold on Thursday and Friday was the same for each day. If the amount for Thursday was 976, what was the total sales of hot dogs for the week? If the amount for Thursday was doubled, what would be the week's total?

2. During yesterday's game at Smallville Stadium, Section A bought 57 hot dogs from the vendor; Section B bought 98 hot dogs; Section C bought 126 hot dogs; and Section D bought 104 hot dogs. How many hot dogs were bought altogether?

3. A vote was taken among all visitors to the stadium last week about what brands of hot dogs they liked. Brand A received 1,908 votes; Brand B received 7,002 votes; Brand C received 2,653 votes; and Brand D received 6,598 votes. What was the total number of visitors to the stadium last week?

4. Schools located near the stadium were invited to bring their classes to exhibition games during the week. For lunch, each student was given a choice of having either a hot dog and a drink, or a hamburger and a drink. On the first day, 376 students had hot dogs. On the second day, 657 students chose hot dogs. On the third day, 208 students chose hot dogs. On the fourth day, only 32 students had hot dogs. On the last day, 860 students had hot dogs. How many students had hot dogs during the week?

5. The hot dogs served at the food stand are shipped from all over the country. One shipment was sent from San Francisco to Los Angeles, a distance of 347 miles. Then it was shipped to New York, which is another 2,451 miles. From New York, it was accidentally shipped to Washington, D.C., 205 miles away. The shipment ended up in Chicago four days late, with an additional 714 miles on it. What was the total mileage the hot dog shipment traveled?

6. The night before the big hot-dog-eating contest, Cindy dreamed she gobbled up 450 hot dogs. Gino dreamed he wolfed down 792. Ana dreamed she stuffed in 1,000 hot dogs. And Jennifer dreamed she managed to eat 2,433 hot dogs. If those wild dreams actually come true, how many hot dogs would have been consumed?

Palindromes are numbers that are the same whether they are read forward or backward. Here are some examples: 7667; 303; 89,098.

A number that is not a palindrome can be turned into one by adding numbers to it. For example, the number 237 is not a palindrome. But you could add its reverse, 732, to it and get 969, which is a palindrome.

Some numbers take longer to make into palindromes; you just have to keep adding the reverse of the previous number. For example:

$$764 + 467 = 1,231$$
$$1,231 + 1,321 = 2,552$$

That's a two-step palindrome. See how many steps it takes to make the numbers below into palindromes.

1. 657 _____   6. 97 _____

2. 379 _____   7. 175 _____

3. 2,096 _____   8. 539 _____

4. 3,578 _____   9. 86 _____

5. 798 _____   10. 192 _____

There is only one place in the United States where one corner from four states comes together. Solve each problem, then find which letter each sum represents. Write those letters on the lines above the matching sums. Then fill in the blanks on your own.

1. 90,786 + 3,568 = _____
2. 90,382 + 2,730 = _____
3. 74,839 + 4,829 = _____
4. 10,293 + 76,859 = _____
5. 4,002 + 38,871 = _____
6. 703 + 907 = _____

7. 374,805 + 29,348 = _____
8. 56,009 + 46,101 = _____
9. 6,749 + 16,274 = _____
10. 73,200 + 3,960 = _____
11. 203,934 + 39,204 = _____
12. 392,038 + 1,920 = _____

1,610 = Z

42,873 = M

243,138 = C

23,023 = R

404,153 = D

87,152 = T

94,354 = U

102,110 = H

393,958 = W

77,160 = L

79,668 = X

93,112 = N

___ ___ ___ ___, ___ ___ ___
94,354 87,152   102,110 93,112   393,958

___ ___ ___ ___ ___ ___,
42,873   79,668   243,138

___ ___ ___ ___ ___ ___ ___,
243,138   77,160   23,023   404,153

___ ___ ___ ___ ___ ___ ___
    23,023   1,610   93,112

A Walk in the Woods

Look at the problems in the boxes. What do you think the answer will be by the time you solve the last problem?

Solve the problems along the path. Write your answers in the blank boxes following each problem. Was your prediction correct?

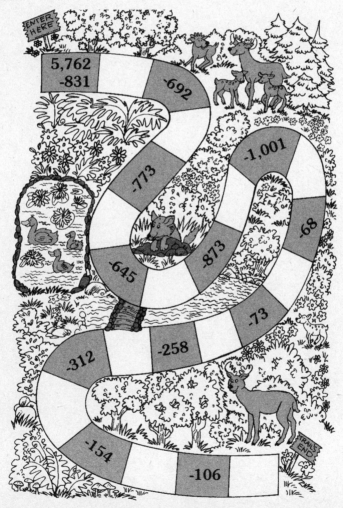

ENTER HERE

5,762
-831

-692

-1,001

-773

-68

-873

-645

-73

-312

-258

-154

-106

TRAIL'S END

Figure out which numbers are missing so the problems can be solved correctly.

1.
```
  7,2_0
  -513
  ─────
  6,777
```

2.
```
   817
  -6_1
  ────
   126
```

3.
```
  4,_29
 -_,875
 ──────
    254
```

8.
```
  96,4_ _
  -7,_51
  ───────
  8_,077
```

4.
```
  2,5_3
  - 69_
  ─────
  1,_24
```

9.
```
  5_,5_5
  - _2,_22
  ───────
  33,33_
```

5.
```
  12,_63
  -_,929
  ──────
  6,7_4
```

10.
```
   _,7_3
  - 2,_68
  ──────
   7,28_
```

6.
```
  14,90_
  -9,_90
  ──────
  _,9_0
```

11.
```
  6,_ _6
  -_,00_
  ──────
  3,883
```

7.
```
  6_,824
  -_2,87_
  ──────
  24,_48
```

12.
```
  3_,9_2
  - 8,_3_
  ──────
  _8,341
```

Find the row in which all the answers equal 634. The row may be across, down, or sideways!

5,902 -5,268	97,165 -96,538	7,697 -7,063	5,327 -5,237	9,870 -8,989
4,080 -3,729	915 -299	9,087 -8,453	12,879 -11,255	29,475 -28,871
56,385 -55,751	789,098 -788,464	75,735 -75,101	82,000 -81,906	132,576 -131,942
4,567 -3,933	26,841 -26,207	9,303 -8,669	5,927 -5,293	587,094 -586,460
85,794 -85,160	46,937 -46,383	74,209 -73,855	49,506 -48,992	98,765 -98,231

See how fast you can do the following problems.

10	18	23	12	19	16
- 4	- 9	- 8	- 7	- 6	- 7

17	14	12	22	13	18
- 8	- 5	- 9	-17	- 4	-12

24	25	27	21	19	11
-12	-16	-18	-12	- 8	- 6

34	30	35	31	37	29
- 8	- 4	- 14	- 7	- 18	- 13

36	39	43	45	40	48
- 16	- 23	- 24	- 16	- 22	- 39

53	55	56	42	50	51
- 35	- 7	- 49	- 33	- 26	- 12

63	66	57	66	41	69
- 6	- 34	- 14	- 49	- 19	- 59

78	73	77	65	71	80
- 9	- 4	- 18	- 48	- 12	- 57

Add 'Em Up—Really Fast!

Multiplication is a fast way to add numbers together. For example, you might want to add

$$5 + 5 + 5 + 5$$

An easier and faster way to get the answer to this problem is to say

$$5 \times 4 = 20$$

The most important part of becoming good at multiplication is to memorize your multiplication tables. Use the test below to practice your skills and see how many problems you can solve in one minute. Then copy the test over (without the answers!) and test yourself again another day.

$8 \times 3 =$	$11 \times 5 =$	$4 \times 4 =$
$6 \times 9 =$	$2 \times 6 =$	$9 \times 4 =$
$2 \times 2 =$	$7 \times 7 =$	$10 \times 10 =$
$7 \times 1 =$	$8 \times 5 =$	$11 \times 1 =$
$6 \times 6 =$	$12 \times 6 =$	$9 \times 7 =$
$10 \times 8 =$	$4 \times 11 =$	$6 \times 11 =$
$4 \times 7 =$	$6 \times 10 =$	$1 \times 1 =$
$5 \times 1 =$	$3 \times 7 =$	$12 \times 8 =$
$11 \times 6 =$	$5 \times 12 =$	$3 \times 8 =$
$9 \times 9 =$	$8 \times 8 =$	$9 \times 1 =$
$3 \times 3 =$	$7 \times 9 =$	$11 \times 8 =$
$8 \times 1 =$	$12 \times 12 =$	$9 \times 12 =$
$10 \times 2 =$	$11 \times 11 =$	$1 \times 6 =$
$9 \times 8 =$	$5 \times 2 =$	$2 \times 9 =$
$12 \times 7 =$	$3 \times 12 =$	$4 \times 5 =$

To further hone your multiplication skills, make up one-minute tests of your own. Trade them with a friend and see how much you can improve each day.

After you have memorized the multiplication tables, you may begin multiplying together numbers with two or more digits. For example, say you wanted to multiply 28 x 2.

Step 1—Set up the problem.

```
  28
x  2
```

Step 2—Multiply the digits in the ones place.
Line the answer up under the problem
as shown on the right.

```
  28
x  2
  16
```

Step 3—Multiply the bottom number, or
multiplier, by the digit in the tens place.
Line the answer up under the problem
as shown on the right.

```
  28
x  2
  16
  40
```

Note: Zero is used as a place holder here

Step 4—Add the two numbers together.

```
   28
 x  2
   16
 + 40
   56
```

After you are comfortable multiplying two or more digits together, you may wish to do multiplication problems in a short form. Here is a faster way to do the above problem.

Step 1—Multiply the digits in the ones
column, placing the 1 in the tens column
and the 6 in the ones column.

```
 1
  28
x  2
   6
```

Step 2—Multiply the multiplier by the digit
in the tens place, which makes 4. Then add
the one that you carried from the ones
column to make 5, and write a 5 in the
tens place of the answer.

```
 1
  28
x  2
  56
```

On a separate piece of paper, solve each of the problems below, first using the long form of multiplying, then the faster short form.

1.   16
    x 8
	2. 35
	    x 6
		3. 23
		    x 9

4.   62
    x 12
	5. 27
	    x 22
		6. 41
		    x 32

A magic square has the same product when the numbers in each row, column, and diagonal are multiplied together. Look at each of the squares below. Multiply each row, column, and diagonal to see which of the squares are magic. Then circle the magic squares.

1.

22	2	16
4	16	11
8	11	8

2.

48	9	4
1	12	144
36	16	3

3.

200	4	80
16	40	100
20	400	8

4.

120	6	12
24	10	36
3	144	20

Division Pays Dividends

Division is a fast way to subtract numbers. For example, you might want to subtract

$$48 - 8 - 8 - 8 - 8 - 8 - 8$$

An easier and faster way to get the answer to this problem is to say

$$48 \div 8 = 6$$

When you divide a number, or a dividend, by another number, or a quotient, you find out how many times the quotient fits into the dividend. For example, $48 \div 6 = 8$ means that 6 will fit into 48 eight times. Or, if you divided 48 into equal piles of 6, each pile would have 8 in it.

Like multiplication, developing your dividing skills depends upon quickly memorizing basic math facts. Use the test below to practice your skills and see how many problems you can solve in one minute. Then copy the test over (without the answers!) and test yourself again another day.

$24 \div 8 =$	$36 \div 6 =$	$66 \div 6 =$
$54 \div 6 =$	$80 \div 8 =$	$81 \div 9 =$
$4 \div 2 =$	$28 \div 7 =$	$9 \div 3 =$
$7 \div 7 =$	$5 \div 1 =$	$8 \div 1 =$

$20 \div 2 =$	$36 \div 3 =$
$72 \div 8 =$	$16 \div 4 =$
$84 \div 12 =$	$36 \div 9 =$
$55 \div 11 =$	$100 \div 10 =$
$12 \div 6 =$	$11 \div 1 =$
$49 \div 7 =$	$63 \div 9 =$
$40 \div 8 =$	$66 \div 6 =$
$72 \div 12 =$	$1 \div 1 =$
$44 \div 4 =$	$96 \div 12 =$
$60 \div 6 =$	$24 \div 3 =$
$21 \div 7 =$	$9 \div 9 =$
$60 \div 5 =$	$88 \div 11 =$
$64 \div 8 =$	$108 \div 9 =$
$63 \div 9 =$	$6 \div 1 =$
$144 \div 12 =$	$18 \div 9 =$
$121 \div 11 =$	$20 \div 4 =$
$10 \div 5 =$	$100 \div 4 =$

After you have become proficient at basic division skills, you may wish to try more difficult division problems. For example, say you wanted to divide 56 by 2.

Step 1—Set up the problem.

divisor → 2⟌56

quotient ↖ ... ↙ dividend

Step 2—See how many times the first number of the dividend can be divided by the divisor. Write this number above the number of the dividend, as shown.

$$\begin{array}{r} 2 \\ 2\overline{)56} \end{array}$$

Step 3—Multiply the divisor and the first number of the quotient together and write the total under the first number of the dividend, as shown.

$$\begin{array}{r} 2 \\ 2\overline{)56} \\ 4 \end{array}$$

Step 4—Subtract the number from the first number of the dividend, as shown.

$$\begin{array}{r} 2 \\ 2\overline{)56} \\ 4 \\ \hline 1 \end{array}$$

Step 5—Bring down the next number of the dividend, as shown. See how many times this new number can be divided by the divisor. Write the number on top of the dividend, as shown.

$$\begin{array}{r} 28 \\ 2\overline{)56} \\ 4\downarrow \\ \hline 16 \end{array}$$

Step 6—Multiply the divisor and the second number of the quotient together and write the total under the dividend, as shown.

$$\begin{array}{r} 28 \\ 2\overline{)56} \\ 4\downarrow \\ \hline 16 \\ 16 \end{array}$$

$$\begin{array}{r} 28 \\ 2\overline{)56} \\ 4\!\!\downarrow \\ \overline{16} \\ 16 \\ \overline{0} \end{array}$$

Step 7—Subtract, as shown. There is no remainder in this problem.

Division problems may also be done in a shorter, faster way.

Step 1—Divide the divisor into the first number of the dividend. Write the number above the first number of the dividend, and carry the leftover amount onto the next number, as shown.

$$2\overline{)5^16}\quad \overset{2}{}$$

Step 2—Divide the divisor into the second number of the dividend. Write the number above the second number of the dividend, as shown.

$$2\overline{)5^16}\quad \overset{28}{}$$

Solve each of the problems below, first using the long form of division, then the faster short form.

1. $8\overline{)248}$ 2. $6\overline{)960}$ 3. $5\overline{)1,055}$

4. $7\overline{)1,176}$ 5. $9\overline{)7,893}$ 6. $10\overline{)1,090}$

If a divisor does not go into a dividend an even number of times, a remainder will be left over. There are three different ways to show a remainder.

This shows that 5 goes into 56 eleven times, with a remainder of 1.

$$\begin{array}{r} 11 \text{ R}1 \\ 5\overline{)56} \\ \underline{5} \\ 06 \\ \underline{5} \\ 1 \text{ R} \end{array}$$

To show a remainder in fraction form, simply put the remainder over the divisor. Thus, 5 goes into 56 eleven and one-fifth times.

$$\begin{array}{r} 11\frac{1}{5} \\ 5\overline{)56} \\ \underline{5} \\ 06 \\ \underline{5} \\ 1 \end{array}$$

To show a remainder in decimal form, add the decimal and as many zeros as necessary until there is no longer a remainder. Thus, 56 divided by 5 equals 11.2.

$$\begin{array}{r} 11.2 \\ 5\overline{)56.0} \end{array}$$

Do the following division problems. Show the remainder for each problem in three different ways.

1. $8\overline{)140}$ 2. $5\overline{)488}$ 3. $8\overline{)474}$

4. $2\overline{)679}$ 5. $8\overline{)2574}$ 6. $4\overline{)258}$

Fractured Fractions

A fraction is a part of a whole. Just about anything can be divided into fractions—an apple, a group of people, even a sheet of paper.

A fraction has two parts: a numerator and a denominator. For example:

$$\frac{3}{4} \begin{array}{l} \text{numerator} \\ \text{denominator} \end{array}$$

The numerator represents the number of parts of the whole in that fraction. The denominator represents the total number of parts the whole can be divided into.

Look at each of the pictures below. Write the fraction for the shaded part of each picture.

1.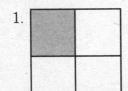

2.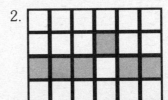

3.

4.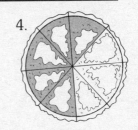

Now draw some pictures to represent the following fractions:

1. $\frac{2}{3}$ 2. $\frac{11}{12}$ 3. $\frac{9}{15}$ 4. $\frac{7}{10}$

5. $\frac{25}{30}$ 6. $\frac{5}{7}$ 7. $\frac{3}{9}$ 8. $\frac{4}{8}$

Equivalent fractions are fractions that represent the same number of parts of the whole. For example, 50 cents may be represented by the following equivalent fractions:

one fifty-cent piece ($\frac{1}{2}$ of a dollar)

two quarters ($\frac{2}{4}$ of a dollar)

five dimes ($\frac{5}{10}$ of a dollar)

ten nickels ($\frac{10}{20}$ of a dollar)

fifty pennies ($\frac{50}{100}$ of a dollar)

Circle the pairs of equivalent fractions below.

| $\frac{3}{4}$ | $\frac{75}{100}$ | | $\frac{3}{4}$ | $\frac{8}{12}$ |

| $\frac{5}{15}$ | $\frac{1}{3}$ | | $\frac{7}{16}$ | $\frac{14}{33}$ |

| $\frac{1}{7}$ | $\frac{2}{21}$ | | $\frac{1}{6}$ | $\frac{4}{24}$ |

| $\frac{1}{10}$ | $\frac{1}{11}$ | | $\frac{5}{6}$ | $\frac{30}{36}$ |

NOTE: Both the numerator and the denominator are multiplied by the same number, or factor, in equivalent fractions.

There are many ways to show the same fraction. For example, $\frac{1}{2}$ is the same as $\frac{4}{8}$, or $\frac{25}{50}$, or $\frac{131}{262}$. If 50 people in a group of 100 have brown eyes, we say that $\frac{1}{2}$ of the people in the group have brown eyes; we don't say that $\frac{50}{100}$ of the people have brown eyes.

By finding the greatest common factor that can be evenly divided into both the numerator and the denominator, any fraction can be reduced to its simplest numbers. *(Note: Not all fractions have a greatest common factor.)*

Find the greatest common factor of the following fractions. Then reduce each fraction down to its simplest numbers. The first one has been done for you.

	Greatest Common Factor	Simplest Fraction
1. $\frac{18}{27}$	9	$\frac{2}{3}$
2. $\frac{9}{12}$		
3. $\frac{15}{35}$		
4. $\frac{12}{64}$		
5. $\frac{27}{29}$		
6. $\frac{8}{22}$		
7. $\frac{121}{132}$		
8. $\frac{16}{88}$		

To compare fractions and determine which is larger, we multiply each fraction so that both denominators are the same. To do this, we choose the least common multiple, which is the smallest number that can be used.

Determine the least common multiple for the following pairs of fractions. The first one has been done for you.

1. $\frac{2}{3}$ __12__   4. $\frac{7}{100}$ ____   7. $\frac{1}{7}$ ____

$\frac{3}{4}$ $\frac{1}{10}$ $\frac{1}{5}$

2. $\frac{7}{8}$ ____   5. $\frac{7}{8}$ ____   8. $\frac{2}{9}$ ____

$\frac{1}{16}$ $\frac{3}{12}$ $\frac{4}{15}$

3. $\frac{3}{5}$ ____   6. $\frac{2}{3}$ ____

$\frac{7}{20}$ $\frac{3}{16}$

Next we multiply each numerator by the factor used to get the least common multiple of the denominator. For example, if the fraction is $\frac{2}{3}$ and the least common multiple is 12, the numerator is multiplied by 4 (3 x 4 = 12). Therefore, $\frac{2}{3}$ may also be expressed as $\frac{8}{12}$.

Convert each of the following fractions so that the denominator is the multiple shown.

1. $\frac{3}{4} = \frac{}{12}$ 5. $\frac{7}{10} = \frac{}{80}$

2. $\frac{7}{9} = \frac{}{27}$ 6. $\frac{2}{3} = \frac{}{15}$

3. $\frac{5}{11} = \frac{}{66}$ 7. $\frac{5}{12} = \frac{}{72}$

4. $\frac{12}{15} = \frac{}{30}$ 8. $\frac{3}{7} = \frac{}{63}$

Like all numbers, fractions can be added and subtracted. However, a special rule applies for adding and subtracting fractions: The denominator of each fraction must be the same, and only the numerators are added. For example:

$$\frac{1}{3} + \frac{1}{3} = \frac{2}{3}$$

$$\frac{1}{3} + \frac{1}{4} \neq \frac{2}{7}$$

In order to add fractions with different denominators, we have to find the least common denominator. For example:

$\frac{1}{3}$ is the same as $\frac{4}{12}$

$\frac{1}{4}$ is the same as $\frac{3}{12}$

We can therefore write:

$$\frac{4}{12} + \frac{3}{12} = \frac{7}{12}$$

On a separate sheet of paper, find the least common denominator in each of the problems below. Convert the fractions, then add or subtract them to get the answers.

1. $\frac{2}{3} + \frac{1}{5} =$

2. $\frac{1}{2} + \frac{3}{6} =$

3. $\frac{1}{13} + \frac{11}{13} =$

4. $\frac{3}{9} + \frac{1}{3} =$

5. $\frac{2}{9} + \frac{2}{6} =$

6. $\frac{3}{4} + \frac{2}{5} =$

7. $\frac{1}{3} + \frac{1}{4} =$

8. $1 - \frac{1}{4} =$

9. $\frac{11}{12} - \frac{2}{3} =$

10. $\frac{5}{4} - \frac{6}{5} =$

11. $\frac{3}{4} - \frac{3}{8} =$

12. $\frac{5}{25} - \frac{1}{5} =$

13. $\frac{7}{10} - \frac{1}{2} =$

14. $\frac{4}{8} - \frac{1}{4} =$

15. $\frac{6}{6} - \frac{2}{5} =$

To multiply a fraction by a whole number, multiply the numerator only by the number. For example:

$$\frac{2}{5} \times 5 = \frac{10}{5} = 2$$

Solve the following multiplication problems. Reduce your answers to lowest terms where possible.

1. $\frac{2}{9} \times 2 =$ 4. $\frac{6}{15} \times 2 =$

2. $\frac{3}{11} \times 4 =$ 5. $\frac{3}{4} \times 3 =$

3. $\frac{9}{14} \times 2 =$ 6. $\frac{3}{10} \times 6 =$

To multiply a fraction by a fraction, multiply the numerators and denominators with each other. For example:

$$\frac{2}{5} \times \frac{1}{5} = \frac{2}{25}$$

Solve the following problems by multiplying the numerators and denominators. Reduce your answers to lowest terms where possible.

1. $1.2 \times \frac{3}{4} =$ 4. $\frac{5}{6} \times \frac{2}{3} =$

2. $\frac{7}{8} \times \frac{1}{8} =$ 5. $\frac{4}{5} \times \frac{1}{2} =$

3. $\frac{3}{4} \times \frac{7}{8} =$ 6. $\frac{5}{9} \times \frac{7}{8} =$

To divide a whole number or a fraction by a fraction, simply multiply the number by the inverse of the fraction. The inverse of a fraction is the fraction "flipped over," placing the numerator on the bottom and the denominator on the top. For example:

$$3 \div \frac{1}{3} \text{ becomes } 3 \times \frac{3}{1} = 9$$

Solve the following problems using this formula. Reduce your answers to lowest terms where possible.

1. $\frac{5}{6} \div \frac{3}{4} =$ 4. $\frac{7}{12} \div 2 =$

2. $\frac{1}{2} \div \frac{8}{3} =$ 5. $8 \div \frac{4}{3} =$

3. $\frac{3}{9} \div 3 =$ 6. $6 \div \frac{1}{7} =$

Explaining Decimals

Here are some important facts about decimals:

*Decimals are forms of fractions.

*Any fraction may be written in decimal form.

*There are place values for decimals just like any number. The place following the decimal point is the tenths place. The next place is the hundredths place. To the right of that is the thousandths place. And to the right of that is the ten thousandths place!

Read these decimals aloud.

.4	.05	.7098
.6	.009	.0003
.12	.94	.50
.02	.124	.1000

Now write these decimals as fractions. To do this, you will need to know what place the last number of the decimal falls in. Write the place value as the denominator. Write the decimal number as the numerator. Then reduce it to its lowest form.

.01 _____		.8012 _____
.20 _____		5.97 _____
2.9 _____		.6002 _____
.50 _____		.1 _____

Write the fractions below in decimal form. One way to do this is to divide the numerator by the denominator. (Don't forget to add the decimal point to the left of the tenths place!) If the denominator is already one of the decimal place values, you can rewrite the number by adding a decimal point before the number and leaving out the denominator.

$\frac{1}{3}$ _____

$\frac{623}{1,000}$ _____

$\frac{1}{2}$ _____

$\frac{5,454}{10,000}$ _____

$5\frac{7}{10}$ _____

$1\frac{6}{100}$ _____

$\frac{41}{100}$ _____

$\frac{2}{5}$ _____

How do you figure out which of these decimals is more and which is less? If the decimals have different place values, you must first convert the decimal with fewer digits to the place value of the decimal with more digits. Figure out which is more. Then convert the decimal back into its original form. Write the symbols for more and less in the blank spaces.

Here is an example:

.3 ____ .06

Convert .3 to .30, then compare .30 to .06. Thirty hundredths is larger than six hundredths. Therefore, the answer is .3 > .06.

Fill in > or < in each of the problems below.

.7 ____ .89

.864 ____ .099

.380 ____ .09

.0768 ____ .7

.1 ____ .01

.2 ____ .2000

.95 ____ .957

.111 ____ .22

The salesman who was supposed to mark sale items with a fraction of the price taken off did it instead with decimals. You only have a few minutes before the doors open to convert each item marked with a decimal to fraction form. Reduce everything to its simplest form.

1. .75 OFF

2. .25 OFF

3. .20 OFF

4. .80 OFF

5. .125 OFF

6. .50 OFF

7. .40 OFF

8. .60 OFF

9. .30 OFF

10. .05 OFF

To answer the following questions, you will need to add and subtract decimals. To do this, just line up the numbers with the decimal points under one another. When subtracting, place the larger number on top. Hint: You may add zeros to the number on top when the number on the bottom has more place values than the number on top.

1. Tammy went to the hardware store for a length of copper wire that measures .2 inches. The store only sells the wire in .5 lengths. How much extra wire will Tammy have?

2. The mechanic has two sections of tubing. One is .57 inches long and the other is .44 inches long. He needs one tube that is .91 inches long. If he combines the two lengths, will he have enough?

3. Phil came in second in a race, finishing .90 seconds behind the first place winner. Ken came in third place, 2.04 seconds behind the first place winner. How much time was there between Ken's time and Phil's time?

4. The school warning bell rang at 8:35 AM. Suzy entered the classroom .44 seconds later. Kyle came in .30 seconds after Suzy. Rob came in .08 seconds after Kyle. How much time passed between the bell ringing and Rob entering the classroom?

5. Mom bought 3.5 pounds of potatoes at the market. Dad bought 7.75 pounds of potatoes. How many pounds of potatoes were bought altogether?

6. Grandma used up 3.2 pounds of the above potatoes cooking the first night, 4.99 the second night, and .75 the third night. How many pounds of potatoes were left for the fourth night?

7. Fran noticed the .5 ounce bottle of perfume had less in it than she expected. She returned the bottle and bought one containing .60 ounces. Still not satisfied, Fran returned that bottle and bought one with .75 ounces. What was the difference in amount each time Fran bought a new bottle?

To multiply decimals, you proceed the same way as you do with whole numbers, then add the decimal point in the product. For example:

$$5 \times .03 = .15$$

Since this equation has a total of two decimal places, the decimal point is moved two places to the left in the final answer (15 becomes .15).

If both numbers are decimals, then the number of decimal places in the first added to the number in the second would tell you how many decimal places are needed in the product. For example:

$$.5 \times .03 = .015$$

In this equation you must move the decimal three places to the left. Since there were only two places in 15, you must add a zero before the number to accommodate the extra decimal place.

Dividing decimals works the same way. When dividing a decimal by a whole number, place the decimal point in the quotient according to how many places are in the decimal. For example:

$$.78 \div 3 = .26$$

When dividing a decimal by a decimal, move the decimal point to the right until the divisor is no longer a decimal, but a whole number. Move the decimal point to the right in the dividend the same number of places. Then continue as if you were dividing a decimal by a whole number. For example:

$$
\begin{array}{r}
0.4 \\
.25 \overline{\smash{)}.100} \\
\underline{100} \\
0
\end{array}
$$

Now try solving these problems using multiplication and division.

1. The home economics class is buying fabric for a sewing project. Each student will need 2.4 yards of fabric. There are 18 students in the class. How many total yards will the class need?

2. There are 6.8 brownies left in the cafeteria's dessert bar, and 10 students want one each. If they divided them equally, how much would each student get?

3. Toni can do her assigned reading fairly quickly. It takes her 1 minute to read 1.75 pages. If the book she is currently reading is 238 pages long, how long will it take her to read it?

4. Gary is a whiz in wood shop. He can saw a board in half in 1.3 minutes. If he needs 15 boards sawed in half for a project, how long will it take him?

5. Mr. Blaze has observed that it takes his students 2.8 minutes to take out their belongings and get settled before work can begin. If he has seven classes a day, and he teaches five days a week, how much time is spent on settling in?

6. The only question Carl got wrong on his math test was

$$.026 \div 8.19$$

Can you tell him the right answer?

7. Camilla was the star basketball player on her school team. She averaged 34.7 points a game. If there were 14 games in the season, how many points did she score altogether?

8. The cafeteria serves 1,030 students a day. Lunch today is macaroni and cheese. If there is 638.6 pounds of it altogether, how much will each student receive on his or her tray?

Numbers can be rounded off to a certain place value. The place value may be to the right or left of the decimal. When we round off a number, we look at the number to the right of the place value designated. If it is for a value of five or above, the number in the place value designated for rounding off is increased by one. If its value is four or under, the number in the place value designated stays the same. For example:

2,354.097 rounded off to the nearest ones = 2,354

or

2,354.097 rounded off to the nearest hundredths = 2,354.10.

The numbers to the right of the designated place value become zeros.

We need to round off numbers for a variety of reasons. For example, when you need to estimate a bill total, it is easier if all the prices are in dollars and not cents.

Round off the following numbers to the place values requested.

1. 7,890,531
to the nearest hundred

2. 57,890.78
to the nearest tenth

3. 69.0456
to the nearest one

4. 5.2890
to the nearest thousandth

5. 128,234,847
to the nearest ten-thousand

6. 46,001.36
to the nearest ten

7. 32,846.002
to the nearest tenth

8. 10.2938
to the nearest thousandth

9. 45.9
to the nearest one

10. 75.7575
to the nearest hundredth

11. 8,309
to the nearest thousand

12. 17
to the nearest ten

You may think of percents in several different ways:

*As ratios, where the second number is 100.

*As decimals to the hundredths place.

*As fractions, where the denominator is 100.

Percentages can be converted back and forth among these three ways.

Here are some examples showing how to convert ratios to percentages. (To reverse, simply discard the percentage symbol and substitute the number into the phrase "_____ out of 100," or simplify it if necessary.)

23 out of 100 = 23%   54 out of 100 = 54%

47 out of 100 = 47%   22 out of 50 = 44 out of 100 = 44%

To convert fractions to percentages, write the denominator as 100 and multiply the numerator by the same amount it took to change the denominator into 100. (To reverse, place the percent over 100 and reduce to simplest forms.)

23/50 = 46/100 = 46%   8/25 = 32/100 = 32%

75/100 = 75%   3/5 = 60/100 = 60%

To convert fractions whose denominators do not divide into 100, divide the numerator by the denominator. Do not go further than the hundredths place and give the remainder, if there is one, as part of the percentage. Here are some percentages that you should try to remember because they are used frequently in everyday life.

1/3 = 33 1/3 %   1/12 = 8 1/3%

1/8 = 12 1/2%   2/3 = 66 2/3%

To convert decimals to percentages, or decimals ending in the tenths place, convert them to the hundredths place by adding a zero, then put the new number over a denominator of 100, and follow the directions for converting fractions to percentages. (To reverse, place the percent over a denominator of 100, then change it back to a decimal by dividing by 100.) Simplify if possible.

.3 = .30 = 30/100 = 30%   .08 = 8/100 = 8%

.98 = 98/100 = 98%   .1 = .10 = 10/100 = 10%

Solve the following percentage problems.

1. The marching band is looking for new members. Right now only 28 of the 70 members are available to perform at the football games. What percent cannot perform?

2. Mary received a 10 out of 10 mark, or 10/10, on a quiz. Robin's grade was 8/10. Bob's grade was 7/10. On the final exam, Mary received a 98/100, Robin received an 85/100, and Bob received a 70/100. Whose percentage of correct answers was identical on both tests?

3. The swim team has won 30% of its meets this season. If there were 10 meets so far, how many have they won?

4. Six of the 30 students in Mr. Bradley's class are consistently late each morning. Fifteen make it with minutes to spare. And three students always come in early to help Mr. Bradley with classroom chores. What percent of the class come late? On time? Early?

5. 280 sixth-graders voted on whether to spend their field day at the museum village learning about pioneer days. 168 students voted no. What percent voted yes?

6. A fund-raiser at school motivated the wood shop students to design and build children's toys. On Monday, they made 15 of the 20 toys they wanted to finish. On Tuesday, they completed 20 of the 25 they started. On Wednesday, 9 out of 10 were finished. On Thursday, 15 out of 25 were made. And on Friday, 40 out of 50 were completed. Write the percent of toys finished for each day.

7. The senior class wanted to spend under $200 on the last party of the year because they had only $203 in the school account. The committee sent a group of students out to comparison shop. In the first store they entered, a pack of 100 balloons cost $8. In the second store, balloons cost $4. In a third store, the amount of soda they wanted to buy would cost them $30. The fourth store would charge them $40 for the soda. Write the fractional form of the ratio of the balloon prices and the soda prices. Convert the prices into percents.

8. The school store ordered too much looseleaf paper. It would like to sell this overstock quickly. The usual price for a package of 50 sheets is 80 cents. To make the sale, they will offer the packages with 1/4 off the usual price. What percent discount are they offering and how much will a package cost with the discount?

9. In Marcy's circle of friends, four have part-time jobs during the week, three have part-time jobs on weekends, and three get allowances from their parents. What percent of friends have jobs during the week? On weekends? Get allowances?

10. Students were encouraged to open savings accounts at the local bank. They were offered an annual 5% interest rate. Sam started his account with $300. Peter started his with $450. How much interest will each of them earn by the end of the year?

Making a Point

A point is a location is space. Points are usually designated with capital letters. For example:

A line is a series of points that extend in opposite directions forever. Lines have no width, but they do have infinite length. Locations on a line are identified by points. Two points can define a line. Lines are designated by showing points with the line symbol above them.

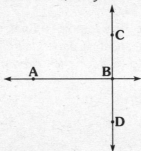

$\overleftrightarrow{AB}$ and $\overleftrightarrow{CD}$ are lines. When naming lines, the order of points does not make a difference. Thus, these lines may also be called $\overleftrightarrow{BA}$ and $\overleftrightarrow{DC}$.

The intersection of these two lines is point B.

Two points within a line define a line segment, which has a finite length.

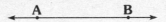

Line segments are named by their points with a line segment symbol over them: $\overline{AB}$.

Because lines are made up of an infinite number of points, there are an infinite number of line segments. Line segments can be the same length or have different lengths. Line segments having the same length are congruent.

A ray is a part of a line that extends infinitely in one direction from a point. It is named by the end point and one other point with the ray symbol.

In this case, naming the points in order is important. The line above is thus $\overrightarrow{AB}$, not $\overrightarrow{BA}$.

The following diagrams include points, lines, line segments, and rays. On a separate sheet of paper, list all possible points, lines, line segments, and rays for each example.

1. 2.

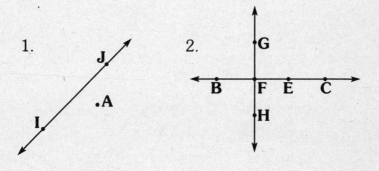

Parallel lines are two lines that never intersect. Since the lines extend to infinity, they must remain exactly the same distance apart at any given point. Here are examples of two parallel lines:

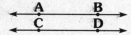

Parallel lines are represented by the symbol //. Thus $\overleftrightarrow{AB}$ // $\overleftrightarrow{CD}$.

If any two lines in the same plane are not parallel, they must intersect at some point. There is a special type of intersection when two lines meet to form a 90° (right) angle. A small box at the intersection indicates a right angle.

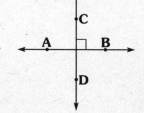

$\perp$ is the symbol for perpendicular lines. Thus $\overleftrightarrow{AB} \perp \overleftrightarrow{CD}$.

On a separate sheet of paper, name the relationships for the following lines.

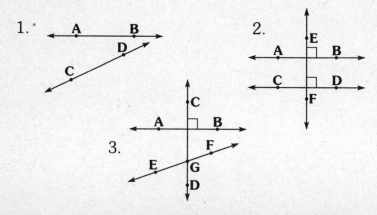

Intersecting lines form angles. Individual angles are formed by two rays that share a common endpoint. This endpoint is called the vertex.

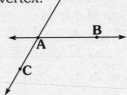

Angles can be named using the angle symbol, <, followed by the three points that form the angle, or by the point that forms the vertex. The angle above could therefore be named <CAB or <A.

Angles are measured using a tool called a protractor. Here are some facts about angles:

*An angle is measured in degrees, from 0° to 180°.

*A 180° angle is a straight line; a 0° angle is a ray.

*An angle formed by perpendicular rays (right angle) is 90°.

*Acute angles are angles that are less than 90°.

*Obtuse angles are angles that are greater than 90°.

Name the following angles, and state whether each is acute, obtuse, or right.

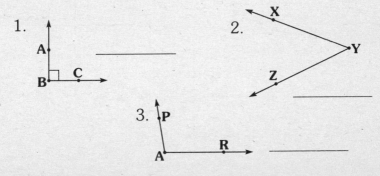

Polygons are shapes in a plane that are formed by three or more line segments. Irregular polygons have sides of unequal lengths and have unequal angles. Regular polygons have sides of equal length and angles of equal sizes.

Polygons are named for their number of sides and shape. Some familiar polygons are:

Triangles

Equilateral—All three sides and all three angles are equal.

Isosceles—Two sides and two angles are congruent (equal).

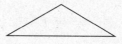

Scalene—All three sides are of different lengths.

Right—A right triangle has one right angle. An isosceles and a scalene triangle may be right triangles as well.

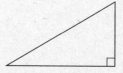

Quadrilaterals

Rectangles—Are formed by four line segments that meet at right angles.

Squares—Are rectangles with all four sides of equal length.

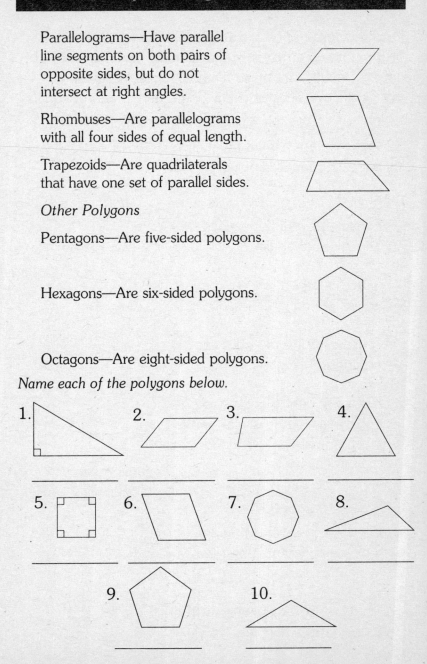

Parallelograms—Have parallel line segments on both pairs of opposite sides, but do not intersect at right angles.

Rhombuses—Are parallelograms with all four sides of equal length.

Trapezoids—Are quadrilaterals that have one set of parallel sides.

Other Polygons

Pentagons—Are five-sided polygons.

Hexagons—Are six-sided polygons.

Octagons—Are eight-sided polygons.

Name each of the polygons below.

1.

2.

3.

4.

_____   _____   _____   _____

5.

6.

7.

8.

_____   _____   _____   _____

9.

10.

_____   _____

Words to Measure By

Find the measurement words hidden in the word search below. Words may be spelled forward, backward, up, down, and diagonally.

acute angle	distance	meter	temperature
area	feet	yard	thermometer
centimeter	height	obtuse angle	volume
circumference	inches	perimeter	weight
degrees	length	pounds	width
depth	liter	radius	miles per hour
diameter	ruler	yardstick	measuring tape

```
K M I L L I M E R T E R T W U N D S T H A U E R O
S P Q U I C T E E F E I H O P O A A N D T L F R T
O O N V E R T H L I W G H U N D R E D S N O O T C
R T O O C I R C U M F E R E N C E N T I M E T E R
C A E B V A M C R A T I A N O N A D M A I T M M O
G A R V T R E T E M A I D R I D T V K P A H I P D
N C A Y R U A O M T H G I E H O N N O O W W L E Y
I U T W E E S E P D O F U T S T U U S L E E E R M
R T S I H L U E H F O E S E H C N I P E U R S A A
E E L L T S R T A R Y M O M C D O T U G A M P T G
T A C A T I I I N N Y A R D S T I C K T H A E U E
E N H E M D N O G A G N R D O N T F O R G E R R H
M G T E T H G I E W N L D D I S T A N C E T H E T
O L T F R E T D J A I C E K I E A N D R W O O S A
M E N N E H A O M T E G I N M P R O V I M E U N T
R F R A S I P E E R R M U R G P H Y D B R O R W N
E A T E M P E R A E T U R E W T H T A T B A T O U
H S A T U R D D E P T H Y N I G H T C A N N O Y O
T O U M A Y N S O T G E T A P Y U P J M E S U R T
```

A polygon is a multi-sided shape. The perimeter of a polygon is the sum of the lengths of the sides. There are a few methods for finding the perimeter of a polygon:

length + width + length + width
    or
(2 x l) + (2 x w)
    or
2 x (l + w)

Only the first method works for quadrilaterals with different length sides. Here is an example:

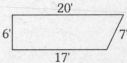

The perimeter of a circle is called the circumference. Here is a formula for finding the circumference.

Circumference = π x diameter

Pi (π) is the symbol used to signify 3.14, or 22/7.

Find the solutions to these perimeter problems.

1. What is the perimeter of the new room that will house the computer department? _____

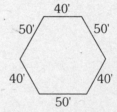

2. The school is planning on building a pool in the basement of the school building. Because of space problems, the pool will have to be made to specific measurements. Look at the architect's drawings and see which one will use the most available space without going over the set perimeter of 250 feet. _____

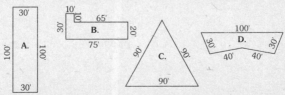

3. If the lengths of all the sides of the weight room are the same, and the perimeter is 72 feet, what is the length of each wall? _____

To find the area of a region, you must find the number of square units in it. Here are some formulas to use when finding the area of some shapes:

Right Triangles—Area = 1/2 x length x width

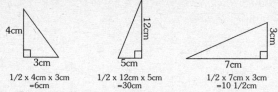

1/2 x 4cm x 3cm
=6cm

1/2 x 12cm x 5cm
=30cm

1/2 x 7cm x 3cm
=10 1/2cm

Other Triangles—Area = 1/2 x base x height

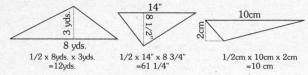

1/2 x 8yds. x 3yds.
=12yds.

1/2 x 14" x 8 3/4"
=61 1/4"

1/2cm x 10cm x 2cm
=10 cm

Parallelograms—Area = base x height

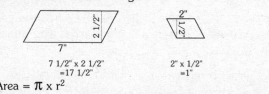

7 1/2" x 2 1/2"
=17 1/2"

2" x 1/2"
=1"

Circles—Area = π x r^2

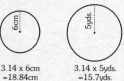

3.14 x 6cm
=18.84cm

3.14 x 5yds.
=15.7yds.

Use 3.14 or 22/7 for π. HINT: If a circle's measurement is given using the diameter rather than the radius, simply divide the diameter by half.

Rectangles—Area = length x width

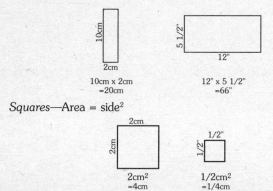

10cm x 2cm
=20cm

12" x 5 1/2"
=66"

Squares—Area = $side^2$

2cm^2
=4cm

1/2cm^2
=1/4cm

Solve the following area problems.

1. The students in Mr. Gray's class were assigned to find the areas of their bedrooms at home. What is the area of Cliff's, Doreen's, and Pam's rooms?

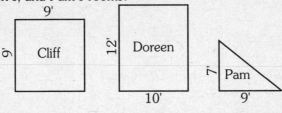

_____   _____   _____

2. Greg's bicycle tire has a diameter of 26 inches. What is the area of the wheel? _____

3. Mrs. Henderson's class baked cookies for the bake sale fund-raiser. Some of the cookies had areas of 12.56 square inches and some had areas of 3.14 square inches. What were the diameters of the cookies? _____

4. The class is giving Ms. Jenkins a farewell party. They need a box with an area of at least 2 square feet to hold the present. Which box will do the job? _____

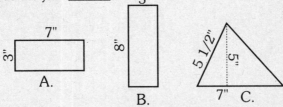

5. The carnival at the school is featuring a contest. If you can guess the correct area of the room with the trick mirrors in it, you will win four passes to Fun Times Amusement Park. Try to figure out the correct area. _____

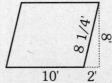

We use a cube to measure volume. The cube measures 1 unit on each side, usually the cubic inch. We can also measure using the cubic foot and yard. To find the volume of a rectangular prism, use the following formula:

Volume = length x width x height

Here are some examples of volume.

7"x7"x 7"=343 cubic inches   2'x1'x9'=18 cubic feet   5 yds. x 6 yds. x 3 yds. = 90 cubic yds.

To find the volume of triangular prisms, use the following formula:

Volume = base x height

Here are some examples of triangular volume:

10' x 6' = 60 cubic feet   10" x 3" = 30 cubic inches

Here are some standard units of measure for liquids:

1 fluid ounce = 2 tablespoons	3 teaspoons = 1 tablespoon
8 fluid ounces = 1 cup	4 tablespoons = 1/4 cup
2 cups = 1 pint	5 1/3 tablespoons = 1/3 cup
4 cups = 1 quart	16 tablespoons = 1 cup
2 pints = 1 quart	4 quarts = 1 gallon

Now try some problems based on volume.

1. What is the volume of these rectangular prisms?

_____   _____   _____

2. If Sam and Sue are baking and they do not have measuring spoons, how can they measure out the 8 tablespoons needed for their recipe?_____

3. Find the volume of these triangular prisms.

_____   _____

Temperature is measured in degrees of Fahrenheit or Celsius.

The Fahrenheit thermometer looks like this:

The Celsius thermometer looks like this:

To convert Fahrenheit degrees to Celsius degrees, use this formula:

Subtract 32° and divide by 1.8.

To convert Celsius degrees to Fahrenheit degrees, use this formula:

Multiply by 1.8 and add 32°.

Here are some standard units of measure for length:

12 inches = 1 foot
3 feet = 1 yard
5,280 feet = 1 mile
1,760 yards = 1 mile

Now try to answer these questions about temperature and length. Round off if necessary.

1. Timmy wrote to his pen pal that the temperature on his vacation stayed about 88°F the whole time. What was the temperature in Celsius degrees?

2. Tony traveled 13 miles on his bicycle round trip. How many yards did he go?

3. Ace can kick a football 76 yards. How many feet is that?

4. Shelley and her family were all set for a vacation in Florida for the month of January. The temperature in Boston was 30°F when they left. The temperature in Florida was 80°F when they arrived. What was the difference in temperature in degrees Celsius?

5. Ron walked 14,080 yards in the walk-a-thon. His brother Jon walked 42,240 feet. Who walked farther?

Many countries use the metric system. The metric system is based on the number 10; each unit is divided into ten equal parts. The units of measurement for length in the metric system are, from smallest to largest:

millimeter
centimeter
decimeter
meter
decameter
hectometer
kilometer

10 millimeters = 1 centimeter	10 decameters = 1 hectometer
10 centimeters = 1 decimeter	10 hectometers = 1 kilometer
10 decimeters = 1 meter	
10 meters = 1 decameter	
1 millimeter = .001 meter	1 decameter = 10 meters
1 centimeter = .01 meter	1 hectometer = 100 meters
1 decimeter = .1 meter	1 kilometer = 1,000 meters

Here are the abbreviations for the metric measurements:

millimeter = mm	decameter = dam
centimeter = cm	hectometer = hm
decimeter = dm	kilometer = km
meter = m	

Other measurements in the metric system are also based on ten. The basic unit for measuring capacity is the liter (1,000 cubic centimeters equals one liter). The basic unit for measuring weight is the kilogram (1,000 milligrams equals one gram). The prefixes remain the same for all units of measurement in the metric system regardless of whether you are measuring length, capacity, or weight.

Here are some examples.

10 milliliters = 1 centiliter	10 grams = 1 decagram
10 centiliters = 1 deciliter	10 decagrams = 1 hectogram
10 deciliters = 1 liter	10 hectograms = 1 kilogram

Answer these questions about the metric system.

1. How many centimeters are in one kilometer? _____

2. How many liters are in one milliliter? _____

3. How many centimeters are in 30 decameters? _____
60 decameters? _____

4. To convert from a larger to a smaller unit in the metric system, all you have to do is move the decimal point to the right. To make a smaller number larger, move the decimal point to the left. Convert these numbers to the unit shown.

93.02 cm = _____mm

123.735 kg = _____grams

38.09 dam = _____m

27.9109 decigrams = _____mg

37 m = _____km

4 dm = _____hm

5. Estimate the weight of the following items. (Hint: one kilogram is equal to a little more than two pounds.) Would they be measured in milligrams, grams, or kilograms?

a. adult _____   b. feather _____

c. paper clip _____   d. soda _____

Reading Graphs

DAY	WEATHER
MONDAY	☀ ☀ ☀ ☁ ☁
TUESDAY	☁ ☁ ☁ ☁ ☁
WEDNESDAY	☀ ☀ ☀ ☀ 🌤 ☁
THURSDAY	☁ ☁ ☁ ☀ 🌤 ☁
FRIDAY	☁ ☁ ☁ ☁ ☁

Key:

 = 8 students think it will be sunny

 = 8 students think it will be cloudy

 = 8 students think it will rain

 = 1 quarter of a picture = 1/4 of 8 students

 = 1 half of a picture = 1/2 of 8 students

Answer the following questions based on the graph above.

1. How many students predicted cloudy weather for Monday? _____ How many predicted sunny weather? _____

2. How many rainy days were predicted? _____
How many students predicted them? _____

3. Which day(s) did the most students participate in the survey? _____

4. Which day(s) had the most varied predictions? _____

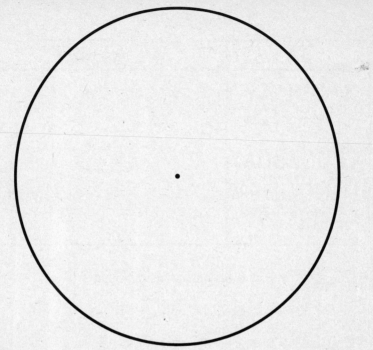

Follow the steps below.

1. Check the closets in your house for the number and styles of shoes your family has.

2. On a sheet of paper, write fractions for the graph using the number of each type of shoe as the numerator and the total number of shoes as the denominator. For example, if there are 12 pairs of shoes and three pairs are sandals, then the fraction would be $\frac{3}{12}$, or $\frac{1}{4}$.

3. Determine the decimal equivalent of each fraction and write it down next to the fractions.

4. Figure out the number of degrees each style of shoes will take up on the graph by multiplying each decimal by 360°. Use a protractor to measure the degrees for each section on the circle above.

5. Color the graph according to shoe type and make a legend to accompany it.

When statistics are taken, the information received can usually be broken down into two modes, or types: categorical and numerical. **Mode** can be used to describe these types of information. It can describe how many students in the school like being a monitor, or it can be used to show what type of car most people like.

When dealing with numbers, median and mean are used. **Median** is used to find the middle of a range of numbers. For example, if everyone in the class wrote down his and her heights and ordered them from shortest to tallest, the exact middle would be the median height of the students in the class. Exactly half would be taller and half would be shorter. If there is no exact middle, then the height between the two middle numbers would be the median.

Mean, or average, is found by adding all the items together and dividing by the number of items.

Solve the problems about mode, median, and mean below.

1. A survey was taken to find out what is an average allowance for a fifth-grader. Here are the responses from Ms. Perez's class: $5.00, $2.00, $1.00, $3.00, $4.00, and $2.50. Find the mean. Round off to the nearest hundredth. _____

2. Two hundred first-graders were asked to tell their favorite vacation spots. The choices given were:
   a. mountains   b. seaside
   c. country   d. city

   Most students chose b. What type of statistic is used to describe this data? _____

3. Here are the weights for the dogs in the pet show: 5 lbs., 2.9 lbs., 86 lbs., 34 lbs., 22 lbs., 12 lbs., 105 lbs., and 71 lbs. What is the median weight of the dogs? _____

4. There were 34 students present when a pop quiz was given. The score results were as follows: 12, 20, 20, 17, 18, 6, 19, 19, 15, 20, 20, and 10. What is the mean score? _____
What is the median score? _____

When in Rome, Do as the Romans Do

The Romans had their own numerical system. The symbols were different from our own Hindu-Arabic numerals but they represented the same amounts we use. And just like our system, the biggest number goes to the left and the other numbers are written to the right.

1 = I	50 = L	1,000 = M	XL = 40	CM = 900
5 = V	100 = C	4 = IV	XC = 90	
10 = X	500 = D	9 = IX	CD = 400	

A bar over a Roman numeral multiplies the value by 1,000. Here are some examples.

$\overline{C}$ = 100,000 $\overline{XC}$ = 90,000

$\overline{MM}$ = 2,000,000 $\overline{CD}$ = 400,000

Convert these Roman numerals to Hindu-Arabic numerals.

1. III _____
2. VI _____
3. LVII _____
4. MDIV _____
5. CLXXV _____

6. CCXXIX _____
7. MMCCXXV _____
8. MCMLXXIV _____
9. XLVI _____
10. XXXVIII _____

Convert these Hindu-Arabic numerals to Roman numerals.

1. 41 _____
2. 9,487 _____
3. 93 _____
4. 1,001 _____
5. 69 _____

6. 283,904 _____
7. 903 _____
8. 117 _____
9. 29,377 _____
10. 7,403 _____

Prime Time

A counting number that has only two factors is a prime number. A counting number that has more than two factors is a composite number. To find the factors of a number, you must see how many pairs of numbers go into it, starting with one.

Here are some examples.

15 = 1 x 15 and 3 x 5, so this must be a composite number

20 = 1 x 20, 2 x 10, and 4 x 5, so this must be a composite number

17 = 1 x 17 only, so this must be a prime number

83 = 1 x 83 only, so this must be a prime number

Find all the factors for each of the following numbers.

1. 4 _____   6. 18 _____

2. 36 _____   7. 27 _____

3. 24 _____   8. 81 _____

4. 55 _____   9. 63 _____

5. 10 _____   10. 9 _____

Are these numbers prime or composite? Write P for prime and C for composite.

1. 1 ____   6. 11 ____

2. 97 ____   7. 67 ____

3. 45 ____   8. 89 ____

4. 6 ____   9. 13 ____

5. 50 ____   10. 29 ____

page 7
1. 265,724—no   2. 230,818—yes   3. 254,754—no
4. 248,172—yes   5. 29,152—yes   6. 250,372—no
7. 266,552—no   8. 298,835—no   9. 326,880—no
10. 204,849—yes

page 8
1. 8,778/10,730   2. 385   3. 18,161   4. 2,133   5. 3,717
6. 4,675

page 9
1. 2 steps   2. 2 steps   3. 1 step   4. 2 steps   5. 4 steps   6. 6 steps
7. 4 steps   8. 4 steps   9. 3 steps   10. 4 steps

page 10
1. 94,354   2. 93,112   3. 79,668   4. 87,152   5. 42,873
6. 1,610   7. 404,153   8. 102,110   9. 23,023   10. 77,160
11. 243,138   12. 393,958
Utah, New Mexico, Colorado, Arizona

page 11
4,931; 4,239; 3,466; 2,821; 1,984; 983; 915; 842; 584; 272;
118; 12

page 12
1. 7,290-513=6,777   2. 817-691=126   3. 4,129-3,875=254
4. 2,523-699=1,824   5. 12,663-5,929=6,734
6. 14,900-9,990=4,910   7. 67,824-42,876=24,948
8. 96,428-7,351=89,077   9. 55,555-22,222=33,333
10. 9,753-2,468=7,285   11. 6,886-3,003=3,883
12. 36,972-8,631=28,341

page 13

The row with answers all equaling 634 is the fourth one down.

page 14

Going across rows:

6	9	15	5	13	9
9	9	3	5	9	6
12	9	9	9	11	5
26	26	21	24	19	16
20	16	19	29	18	9
18	48	7	9	24	39
57	32	43	17	22	10
69	69	59	17	59	23

page 16

1. 128   2. 210   3. 207   4. 744   5. 594   6. 1,312

page 17

2 and 3 are magic squares.

page 21

1. 31   2. 160   3. 211   4. 168   5. 877   6. 109

page 22

1. 17 R4; $17\frac{4}{8}$; 17.5   2. 97 R3; $97\frac{3}{5}$; 97.6
3. 59 R2; $59\frac{2}{8}$; 59.25   4. 339 R1; $339\frac{1}{2}$; 339.5
5. 321 R6; $321\frac{6}{8}$; 321.75   6. 64 R2; $64\frac{2}{4}$; 64.5

page 23

1. $\frac{1}{4}$ 2. $\frac{6}{24}$ 3. $\frac{9}{18}$ 4. $\frac{5}{8}$

page 24

Pairs of equivalent fractions: $\frac{3}{4} - \frac{75}{100}$; $\frac{5}{15} - \frac{1}{3}$;
$\frac{1}{6} - \frac{4}{24}$; $\frac{5}{6} - \frac{30}{36}$

page 25

	Greatest Common Factor	Simplest Fraction
2. $\frac{9}{12}$	3	$\frac{3}{4}$
3. $\frac{15}{35}$	5	$\frac{3}{7}$
4. $\frac{12}{64}$	4	$\frac{3}{16}$
5. $\frac{27}{29}$	1	$\frac{27}{29}$
6. $\frac{8}{22}$	2	$\frac{4}{11}$
7. $\frac{121}{132}$	11	$\frac{11}{12}$
8. $\frac{16}{88}$	8	$\frac{2}{11}$

page 26

2. 16   3. 20   4. 100   5. 24   6. 48   7. 35   8. 45

1. $\frac{9}{12}$ 2. $\frac{21}{27}$ 3. $\frac{30}{66}$ 4. $\frac{24}{30}$ 5. $\frac{56}{80}$ 6. $\frac{10}{15}$ 7. $\frac{30}{72}$ 8. $\frac{27}{63}$

page 27

1. $\frac{13}{15}$ 2. 1   3. $\frac{12}{13}$ 4. $\frac{6}{9}$ 5. $\frac{10}{18}$ 6. $\frac{23}{20}$ 7. $\frac{7}{12}$

8. $\frac{3}{4}$ 9. $\frac{3}{12}$ 10. $\frac{1}{20}$ 11. $\frac{3}{8}$ 12. 0   13. $\frac{2}{10}$ 14. $\frac{2}{8}$

15. $\frac{13}{30}$

page 28

1. $\frac{4}{9}$ 2. $1\frac{1}{11}$ 3. $1\frac{2}{7}$ 4. $\frac{4}{5}$ 5. $2\frac{1}{4}$ 6. $1\frac{4}{5}$

1. $\frac{9}{10}$ 2. $\frac{7}{64}$ 3. $\frac{21}{32}$ 4. $\frac{5}{9}$ 5. $\frac{2}{5}$ 6. $\frac{35}{72}$

1. $1\frac{1}{9}$ 2. $\frac{3}{16}$ 3. $\frac{1}{9}$ 4. $\frac{7}{24}$ 5. 6   6. 42

page 29

$\frac{1}{100}$; $\frac{20}{100}$ or $\frac{1}{5}$; $2\frac{9}{10}$; $\frac{50}{100}$ or $\frac{1}{2}$; $\frac{8,012}{10,000}$; $5\frac{97}{100}$; $\frac{6,002}{10,000}$; $\frac{1}{10}$

page 30

.33; .5; 5.7; .41; .623; .5454; 1.06; .4

.7 < .89   .864 > .099
.380 > .09   .0768 < .7
.1 > .01   .2 = .2000
.95 < .957   .111 < .22

page 31

1. $\frac{3}{4}$ 2. $\frac{1}{4}$ 3. $\frac{1}{5}$ 4. $\frac{4}{5}$ 5. $\frac{1}{8}$ 6. $\frac{1}{2}$
7. $\frac{2}{5}$ 8. $\frac{3}{5}$ 9. $\frac{3}{10}$ 10. $\frac{1}{20}$

page 32

1. .3 inches   2. yes   3. 1.14 seconds
4. .82 seconds   5. 11.25 pounds   6. 2.31 pounds
7. .10 ounces; .15 ounces

page 34

1. 43.2 yds.   2. .68 of a piece   3. 136 minutes
4. 19.5 minutes   5. 98 minutes   6. 315   7. 485.8 points
8. .62 pound

page 35

1. 7,890,500   2. 57,890.8   3. 69   4. 5.289
5. 128,230,000   6. 46,000   7. 32,846   8. 10.294
9. 46   10. 75.76   11. 8,000   12. 20

pages 37-38

1. 60%   2. Bob's   3. 3   4. 20%; 50%; 10%   5. 40%
6. Monday—75%; Tuesday—80%; Wednesday—90%;
Thursday—60%; Friday—80%   7. 8/4 = 200%; 30/40 = 75%
8. 25%; 60 cents   9. 40%; 30%; 30%   10. Sam—$15;
Peter—$22.50

page 40

Points—A, B, C, E, F, G, H, I, J
Lines—BC (or BF, BE, FE, FC, EC); GH (or GF, FH); IJ
Line Segments—BF, BE, BC, FE, FC, EC, GF, GH, FH, IJ
Rays—BC, FC, EC, CB, EB, FB, GH, FH, FG, HG, IJ, JI

page 41

1. intersecting lines   2. $\overleftrightarrow{AB}$ // $\overleftrightarrow{CD}$; $\overleftrightarrow{AB} \perp \overleftrightarrow{EF}$; $\overleftrightarrow{CD} \perp \overleftrightarrow{EF}$
3. $\overleftrightarrow{AB} \perp \overleftrightarrow{CD}$; $\overleftrightarrow{CD}$ intersects $\overleftrightarrow{EF}$ at G; $\overleftrightarrow{AB}$ and $\overleftrightarrow{EF}$ are intersecting lines

page 42

1. <ABC; <B; right angle   2. <XYZ; <Y; acute angle
3. <PAR; <A; obtuse angle

page 44

1. right triangle   2. parallelogram   3. trapezoid   4. equilateral
triangle   5. square   6. rhombus   7. octagon   8. scalene
triangle   9. pentagon   10. isosceles triangle

page 45

```
KMILLIMERTERTWUNDSTHAUERO
SPQUICTEEFEIHOPOAANDTLFRT
OONVERTHLIWGHUNDREDSNOOTC
RTOOCIRCUMFERENCENTIMETER
CAEBVAMCRATIANONADMAITMMO
GARVTRETEMAIDRIDTVKPAHIPD
NCAYRUAOMTHGIEHONNOOWWLEY
IUTWEESEPDOFUTSTUUSLEEERM
RTSIHLVEHFOESEHCNIPEURSAA
EELLTSRTARYMOMCDOTUGAMPTG
TACATIIINNYARDSTICKTHAEUE
ENHEMDNOGAGNRDONTFORGERRH
MGTETHGIEWNLDDISTANCETHET
OLTFRETDJAICEKIEANDRWOOSA
MENNEHAOMTEGINMPROVIMEUNT
RFRASIPEERRMURGPHYDBRORWN
EATEMPERAETUREWTHTATBATOU
HSATURDDEPTHYNIGHTCANNOYO
TOUMAYNSOTGETAPYUPJMESURT
```

page 46

1. 270 feet   2. D—200 feet   3. 72 feet

page 48

1. 81 sq ft; 120 sq. ft; 31.5 sq. ft.   2. 530.66 sq. in.
3. 2 in.; 4 in.   4. Box B   5. 80 sq. ft.

page 49

1. $4\frac{1}{2}$ cubic in.; 8 cubic ft.; 540 cubic ft.   2. $\frac{1}{2}$ cup
3. 28 cubic ft.; 12 cubic in.

page 50

1. 31° C   2. 22,880 yds.   3. 228 feet   4. 25.6 degrees
5. Each walked the same distance (8 miles)

page 52
1. 100,000 cm   2. .001 liter   3. 30,000 and 60,000
4. 930.2 mm; 123,735 g; 380.9 m; 2,791.09 mg; .037 km; .004 hm
5. a is kilograms; b is milligrams; c is milligrams; d is grams

page 53
1. 12 cloudy; 24 sunny   2. 3 days-28 on Tues., 8 on Thurs.,
and 32 on Fri.   3. Wed./Thurs.   4. Thurs.

page 55
1. $2.92   2. mode   3. 28 lbs.   4. mean—16.3;
median—18 1/2

page 56
1. 3   2. 6   3. 57   4. 1,504   5. 175   6. 229   7. 2,225
8. 1,974   9. 46   10. 38

1. XLI   2. $\overline{\text{IX}}$CDLXXXVII   3. XCIII   4. MI
5. LXIX   6. $\overline{\text{CCLXXXIII}}$CMIV   7. CMIII
8. CXVII   9. $\overline{\text{XXIX}}$CCCLXXVII   10. $\overline{\text{VII}}$CDIII

page 57
1. 1 x 4; 2 x 2   2. 1 x 36; 2 x 13; 3 x 12; 4 x 9; 6 x 6
3. 1 x 24; 2 x 12; 3 x 8; 4 x 6   4. 1 x 55; 5 x 11
5. 1 x 10; 2 x 5   6. 1 x 18; 2 x 9; 3 x 6   7. 1 x 27; 3 x 9
8. 1 x 81; 3 x 27; 9 x 9   9. 1 x 63; 3 x 21; 7 x 9
10. 1 x 9; 3 x 3

1. p   2. p   3. c   4. c   5. c   6. p   7. p   8. p   9. p   10. p